Happy Mother's Day 84
Danny

Rodale's *High Health* Cookbook Series

SOUPS
SUPREME

Rodale's High Health *Cookbook Series*

SOUPS SUPREME

by the Editors of Rodale Books

Series Editorial Director:
Charles Gerras

Text Preparation:
Camille Cusumano and Carol Munson

Recipe Research and Editing:
Camille Bucci

Illustrations:
Susan Rosenberger

Art Director:
Karen A. Schell

Series Designer:
Jerry O'Brien

Book Layout:
Linda Jacopetti

Copy Editing:
Jan Barckley

Cover Photography:
Margaret Smyser

Food Stylist:
Kay Seng Lichthardt

Rodale Press, Emmaus, Pennsylvania

Printed in the United States of America on recycled paper, containing a high percentage of de-inked fiber.

On the cover: Hearty Vegetable Soup with Dumplings (for recipe, see page 30).

The recipes in this book have appeared in other Rodale publications.

Library of Congress Cataloging in Publication Data
Main entry under title:

Soups supreme.

(Rodale's high health cookbook series; v. 4) Includes index.
1. Soups. I. Rodale Books. II. Series.
TX757.S636 1983   641.8'13   82-23042
ISBN 0-87857-394-1   hardcover

2 4 6 8 10 9 7 5 3 1   hardcover

Contents

The Simple Magic of Soups

*T*hrough the ages, a steaming kettle of soup has come to symbolize the most basic kind of nourishment. What could be more fundamentally satisfying and healthy than a bowl of soup served with a thick slice of whole-grain bread and a green salad?

The very essence of soup is comfort, and that stems from its role in olden days when times were lean. A brewing pot of soup made from some bare bones, a few vegetables, and perhaps some grains, was a welcome reward at the end of a long day's toil. It restored spirits as few things could.

It is no wonder that eating homemade soup is almost universally accepted as a valuable health measure. Just about everybody has grown up with a special soup recipe patented by grandmother as a cure for all ills. Usually committed to memory rather than to paper, this special blend indeed seemed to have true healing powers. Furthermore, it tasted so good that a bowl of that soup was a treat even when you felt just fine.

How could it be otherwise, when grandmother's soups were made only with fresh, wholesome ingredients? Trading the good taste and nourishment of homemade soup for the promised convenience of one that comes in a can simply wouldn't have made sense to her.

Today we know the secret behind this delicious dish that has the enviable ability to repair the body and soothe the spirit. It is the restorative powers of the nutrients in such ingredients as whole grains, legumes, and fresh vegetables. You will rediscover the satisfaction of these health-giving blends when you follow the same time-tested guidelines of old-fashioned soup cooking.

Besides the nourishment it provides, another big bonus of soup making is the creativity it permits each individual cook. There are no rigid rules for making good soups. Many of the best are the cooks' own inventions. You need only bear in mind that the end result will be as healthful and tasty as the ingredients that initially go into the soup pot.

Soup is not only nourishing, it is also economical. The main ingredients used in soup making are inexpensive. A little meat, poultry, or fish boosted by the goodness of grains, legumes, or dairy products goes a long way in a soup—*and* all without skimping on the nutrition. A few cooked meat bones (after they've been picked clean), or those you buy raw from the butcher for pennies, can give flavor, body, and nutrition to a whole pot of soup.

The versatility of soups is reflected in the numerous types made today. In contrast to their traditional image, soups aren't necessarily hearty, nor must they be hot. Sometimes a chilled fruit or vegetable soup provides just the kind of nourishment you need. Thin broths, or cream or pureed soups, are sometimes more desirable as appetizers that balance out the nutritional and aesthetic demands of your meal. Light or rich, thin or thick, many of the best soups are based on a good nutritious stock.

STOCKS

The difference between a good soup and a great one may lie in the stock used. Stocks are also called *fonds de cuisine*, which means, appropriately enough, "foundations of cooking." Many delicate sauces rely on the concentrated flavor of a stock. Casseroles and stews may also be based upon a stock. Served as a broth with a garnish of croutons, a stock can stand alone as a savory pleasure. An added bonus of stocks for dieters is that they are high in flavor but low in calories. However, the best news for health-conscious people is that stocks contain the nutritional goodness extracted from the stockpot ingredients through long, slow cooking.

Good taste and nutrition are not the only good reasons for making your own stock; the ease of doing it is another. Stock requires some cooking time, but once it is cooking, you can allow it to simmer on its own while you do something else. You need only check it from time to time to make sure it does not boil.

The long, slow cooking is important. First of all, it encourages the meat bones to give up their natural gelatin, adding body, flavor, and nutrition to the stock. The reason for keeping a stock from boiling is to minimize the accumulation of albuminous scum, a protein substance secreted by meat bones. You may remove this scum by skimming the surface of the stock with a slotted spoon during the first 30 minutes of cooking. Keep your simmering stock totally or at least partially uncovered, so you can be sure it does not boil. Some cooks also recommend controlling the temperature by putting an asbestos heating pad over the burner.

Stocks are sometimes referred to as *white* or *brown*, depending on the type of meat bones used. Beef bones (sometimes browned first) will naturally yield a brown stock, while veal and chicken bones make a white one. Brown stocks are most often called for when a very hearty soup or a rich sauce is desired. For a lighter cream soup or sauce, a white stock would be the choice.

Vegetable and fish stocks are even easier to make than meat stock. They require much less cooking time and skimming—for a vegetable stock, there is no need to skim at all. Poultry and veal stocks require two to three hours of simmering, and brown stocks a little longer; fish and vegetable stocks may require as little as a half hour of cooking time.

FILLING THE STOCKPOT

Fill the stockpot with all the solid ingredients before adding cold water to cover all. When buying bones from the butcher, have them chopped into small pieces so they fit easily into the pot, and to expose their good inner properties. Any cooked or uncooked bones with some meat remaining will also make good soup bones, but best results come from bare bones and an inexpensive piece of stew meat. The bones provide the natural gelatinous quality that gives the stock body.

Beef, chicken, and veal bones may all be combined to make a rich stock. The dominating flavor in this case will be beef, but chicken adds a subtle flavor of its own, and veal bones enhance texture, as they are extremely gelatinous. A white stock should be made with only veal or chicken bones.

Chicken stock may be made from all parts of the chicken—wing tips, carcasses (raw or cooked), gizzards, hearts, backs, and necks. Never use the liver for chicken stock; it gives off an unpleasant flavor and darkens the stock.

A brown stock may also be made by browning the stock elements before adding them to the water. This caramelizes the vegetables and meat juices. To make a brown stock, place beef or veal bones in a roasting pan in a hot oven (425°F) for an hour, or until nicely colored. Transfer the bones to the stockpot and deglaze the pan by removing any fat and leaving the juices behind. Scrape the caramelized particles from the bottom, adding water if necessary, and add all this to the stockpot.

Because fish bones have less gelatin than meat bones, the stock will have less body, but it will be just as flavorful. Fish stocks also require less skimming than do meat stocks. Many seafood chowders and stews benefit immensely from a good hearty fish stock.

Fish heads, carcasses, and trimmings of lean white fish can all be used, but freshness is essential. Fatty or oily fish, such as salmon, mackerel, or herring, should never be used. Do not cook a fish stock longer than the recipe calls for, or a bitter taste may result.

To make a simple vegetable stock, use any combination of fresh vegetables. Keep in mind that strong-flavored vegetables, such as asparagus, broccoli, cabbage, and turnips, yield strong broth and are best used sparingly. Starchy vegetables, such as corn, peas, and potatoes, will cloud the liquid if used in too large a quantity. Parsnips and carrots sweeten the liquid. You may use these same guidelines when choosing vegetables to flavor meat stocks. The vegetables most commonly used to flavor meat stocks are carrots, onions, leeks, and celery, along with a *bouquet garni*—a mixture of spices and herbs.

It is not necessary to peel the vegetables for a stock, but they should be well scrubbed and have any blemishes removed. Cut the vegetables in large pieces; small pieces will mush and disintegrate, clouding the stock. Leftover vegetable trimmings are equally flavorful and may be added to the stock. For more intense flavor, saute vegetables lightly in a little butter or oil before adding them to the stock.

STRAINING

Straining separates the tasty, nutritious stock liquid from the solid ingredients after the long simmering has extracted all their goodness. To strain a stock, line a large sieve or colander with a damp, loosely woven cloth, and place over a clean bowl or pan. Ladle the broth into the strainer, and wash out the pot used to cook the stock. The strained stock

may then be returned to the pot for further reducing, and the solid ingredients discarded.

REDUCING STOCK

Reducing stock concentrates its body and flavor into a smaller volume that requires less storage space. To reduce stock, boil it vigorously, uncovered, until the volume is lessened by one-third to one-half. Skim if necessary. Before refrigerating the reduced stock, allow it to cool, but do so as quickly as possible to prevent bacterial growth.

STORING STOCKS

Store the cooled stock in covered containers at once. It will keep under refrigeration for about a week. If you wish to have stock on hand longer than that, freeze it in small covered containers or in ice-cube trays. The frozen cubes can be unmolded and stored in sealed plastic bags to be used as needed, without defrosting a large quantity of stock. Label and date the stock you freeze. It will keep for up to a year. Before using any stock that has been frozen, bring it to a full rolling boil. Soups should be stored with the same precautions as stocks. Soups made with cream, milk, or eggs should not be kept for longer than two days. All soups may be frozen. As with stock, reheat to the boiling point to kill any harmful bacteria.

Beef Stock

1 beef shin or soup bone

2 carrots, cut in chunks

2 stalks celery, with leaves, cut in chunks

2 medium-size onions, cut in chunks

8 cups cold water

In a 4-quart heavy-bottom soup pot, brown beef bone well, then carrots, celery, and onions.

Add water, cover with a tight-fitting lid, and simmer over very low heat 3 hours. Strain the stock, discard bone and vegetables, cool the stock, and then refrigerate. Before using stock, remove the surface fat.

Yields about 6 cups

To cool a stock quickly so that you can skim the fat from the surface, place the entire pot in a larger basin or bowl, surround it with ice, stir the broth until it is completely cool, then let it set so that the fat can rise. Another way to accomplish this is to set the pot on blocks in a sink filled with cold water.

3 pounds chicken backs, necks, and wings, or 1 or 2 turkey backs

1 medium-size onion, quartered

1 stalk celery, with leaves

Poultry Stock

Place chicken or turkey in a 6-quart soup pot. Add enough water to cover, onion, and celery, and slowly bring to a boil. Reduce heat and slowly simmer, covered, 2 hours.

Remove from heat, strain, cool, and refrigerate. When the stock is cool, remove the surface fat.

Yields about 5 cups

Consomme

Consomme is prepared from a basic stock, clarified with egg whites and crushed egg shells. Place degreased cold stock in a 4-quart enamel or stainless-steel pot and slowly heat until warm. Whisk egg whites and crushed shells into the warm stock so that they come in contact with all the liquid in the pot, then let them rise to the top. Lower the heat and allow the stock to simmer until clear (5 to 10 minutes). To check clarity of stock, gently push the coagulated egg whites aside. Place a strainer lined with a clean wet dishcloth over a deep bowl. Carefully pour the clarified stock through the strainer.

2 pounds fish heads, backs,
and bones

6 cups water

juice of 1 large lemon

2 large onions, quartered

3 stalks celery, quartered

Fish Stock

3 carrots, quartered

1 bay leaf

10 peppercorns

3 sprigs parsley

1 sprig thyme

*P*lace all ingredients in a 5-quart soup pot. Bring to a boil, lower heat, and simmer, uncovered, 30 minutes. Skim the surface if necessary.

Soak a 3-layer piece of cheesecloth in cold water and wring it out. Strain the stock through the cheesecloth into another large, clean pot.

Cool the strained stock, and refrigerate or freeze until needed. If large fish heads are used, remove the meat to use in fish soup or salad.

Note: A richer stock may be made by increasing the cooking time.

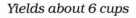

Yields about 6 cups

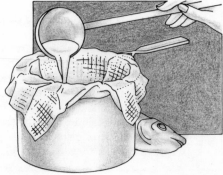

5 large onions, halved

10 carrots

8 tomatoes, quartered

1 clove garlic, minced

5 stalks celery

1 bunch parsley

16 cups water

Vegetable Stock

Combine ingredients in a 6- to 8-quart soup pot. Bring to a boil, reduce heat to low, cover, and simmer 1 hour.

Let sit 30 minutes and then strain. Skim any scum that may form.

Yields 16 cups

Garlic Stock

Garlic stock is a savory liquid that may be used as a base for tomato or vegetable soups. Lengthy cooking subdues the garlic's pungency without diminishing its distinct flavor. A large head of garlic will subtly season 8 cups of stock. Simmer the garlic—unpeeled, crushed cloves—along with any other vegetables desired for about 1 hour. Strain before storing or serving.

FULL-MEAL SOUPS

*T*he comfort a warm bowl of hearty homemade soup can provide is immeasurable. Everybody has a favorite for those bad-weather days, and for when the colds season threatens. Some soups seem to contain just about everything you need to stay healthy.

Full-meal soups are so well esteemed because they offer the hearty satisfaction a person yearns for after a hard day's work. Sometimes a thick, rich soup is the simplest way for a busy mother to ensure proper nutrition for the whole family with a single dish. It contains all the goodness so often lost from meats and vegetables prepared other ways. Except for vitamin C and some B vitamins, which are especially sensitive to heat, nothing of value escapes the soup pot.

If full-meal soups based on meat, poultry, or fish are solidly good nourishment—and they certainly are that—it's a marvelous bonus. The obvious truth is that they are, first of all, splendid treats guaranteed to please many tastes, with a variety of flavors and textures that stand up to the demands of most any crowd.

1½ cups white beans

1 medium-size meaty beef
    bone

6 cups cold water

1 cup coarsely chopped celery

1 large carrot, chopped

1 medium-size onion, chopped

1 clove garlic, minced

1 tablespoon oil

¼ teaspoon freshly ground
    pepper

1 tablespoon coarsely
    chopped parsley

Bean Soup

*W*ash beans and cover with cold water. Refrigerate, covered, overnight.

Next day, using a 4-quart soup pot, combine beans and liquid with beef bone and 6 cups water. Place pot over medium heat and bring to a boil. Reduce heat, cover, and simmer.

Add celery and carrot to soup. Saute onion and garlic in oil and then add to soup mixture. Stir and simmer, covered, 1½ hours, or until beans are very tender. Season with pepper during last hour of cooking.

Remove beef bone. Cut off meat and return it to soup. Before serving, garnish soup with freshly chopped parsley.

Serves 4 to 6

Beef-Barley Soup

1 tablespoon oil

½ pound lean chuck roast, cut into 1-inch cubes

1 1-pound beef soup bone

6 cups cold water

2 tablespoons chopped parsley

2 tablespoons paprika

2 peppercorns

1 or 2 whole allspice

¼ cup barley

½ cup chopped celery, with leaves

¼ cup chopped onions

½ cup diced carrots

1 cup chopped, cooked tomatoes

chopped parsley for garnish

*H*eat oil in a heavy 6-quart soup pot over medium heat and lightly brown beef cubes and soup bone. Add water and bring to a boil. Skim surface scum. Add parsley, paprika, peppercorns, and allspice. Reduce heat to low, cover, and simmer 30 minutes.

Meanwhile, check barley and remove any foreign particles. Add to soup. Stir in celery, onions, and carrots. Cover and simmer over low heat 1 hour.

Add tomatoes and continue to simmer 15 minutes longer. Remove soup bone. Serve garnished with parsley.

Serves 4 to 6

1½ pounds lean beef, cubed

8 cups Beef Stock or Poultry Stock (see Index)

2 bay leaves

1 clove garlic, minced

1 teaspoon tamari soy sauce

1½ cups shredded raw beets

beet tops, if available, chopped

1 cup grated carrots

1 cup grated turnips

1 medium-size onion, chopped

2 tablespoons tomato paste

2 tablespoons lemon juice

1 teaspoon honey

2 cups shredded cabbage

Borscht

*I*n a 6-quart soup pot, combine beef cubes, stock, bay leaves, and garlic. Simmer 40 minutes.

Add the rest of the ingredients and simmer, covered, 25 minutes longer.

Serve in deep bowls with sour cream, yogurt, or tofu.

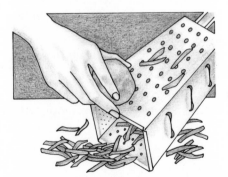

Serves 4 to 6

Bourride *with* Aioli
(Fish Soup with Garlic Mayonnaise)

2 pounds assorted fish (cod, flounder, bass, or others)

1 onion, sliced

1 bay leaf

1 teaspoon dried fennel

1 teaspoon dried thyme

2 cloves garlic, minced

1 piece orange peel

4 tomatoes, peeled, seeded, and quartered

8 cups water or Fish Stock (see Index)

pepper to taste

Aioli:

3 or 4 cloves garlic

1 egg

1 tablespoon lemon juice or vinegar

1 cup olive oil or other vegetable oil

*C*ut fish in pieces. Place in a soup pot with all other ingredients except *aioli* and cook over medium heat 10 to 15 minutes, or until fish is done.

To make the *aioli*, chop garlic and place in a blender with egg and lemon juice or vinegar. Blend for a few seconds. Then slowly add oil in a thin stream, while still blending, until all the oil is incorporated.

Strain soup. Slowly stir a third of the *aioli* into soup. Serve over slices of French bread. Fish may be served separately or with soup, along with rest of *aioli.*

Serves 12

2 medium-size onions, sliced

4 tablespoons oil

2 cups coarsely shredded
     cabbage, turnip greens, or
     Swiss chard

2 cups grated carrots

1 cup chopped apples

5 cups Beef Stock (see Index)

2 tablespoons tomato paste

⅓ cup brown rice

½ cup coarsely chopped cashews

½ cup raisins

1 to 1½ cups yogurt

Cashew-Carrot Soup

*I*n a Dutch oven or 6-quart heavy-bottom soup pot, saute onions in oil. Stir in greens and saute a few minutes longer. Then add carrots and cook 1 to 2 minutes longer. Stir in apples, stock, and tomato paste. Bring the mixture to a boil and add rice. Simmer, covered, 35 to 40 minutes, or until carrots are tender and rice is cooked.

Add cashews and raisins and cook until raisins are "plumped." Serve each bowl of soup topped with a generous dollop of yogurt.

Serves 4 to 6

Cheddar Cheese Soup

1 cup whole wheat bread cubes

¾ cup cubed Cheddar cheese

1½ cups skim milk

2 teaspoons Dijon-style mustard

few grains of cayenne pepper

*P*lace bread cubes, a few at a time, in a blender and process with short bursts on high speed to obtain crumbs. Or, alternatively, crumble the bread cubes into crumbs by hand.

Place the bread crumbs with the remaining ingredients in a medium-size saucepan and cook over medium heat, stirring constantly, until the mixture comes to a boil. Reduce heat and continue to stir until the cheese is melted and the mixture is well blended and smooth (about 5 to 6 minutes). Serve hot.

Serves 2

Note: Other cheeses, such as longhorn, can be substituted for Cheddar.

3 tablespoons olive oil

1 large onion, finely chopped

2 stalks celery, finely chopped

2 cloves garlic, finely chopped

1 pound boneless, skinned
   chicken breast, cubed

3 tomatoes, diced

1 medium-size potato, cubed

5 cups Poultry Stock (see Index)

½ pound green beans, cut into
   1-inch pieces

½ cup corn (1 ear)

1 medium-size zucchini, diced

1 sweet red pepper, chopped

2 tablespoons chopped parsley

Chunky Calico Chicken Soup

*H*eat oil in a 3-quart soup pot. Add onion and celery and saute 5 minutes over medium heat. Add garlic and chicken and saute, while stirring, 5 minutes longer. Add tomatoes, potato, and stock and bring to a boil. Lower heat, cover, and simmer 15 minutes.

Add green beans, cover, and cook 5 minutes longer.

Add corn, zucchini, and pepper and cook an additional 5 minutes. Stir in the parsley. Serve hot.

Serves 6

3 pounds beef shoulder or
country-style ribs

1 beef soup bone

1 large onion or 2 leeks,
chopped

16 cups water

3 cups kale

1 large bunch parsley

2 stalks celery

4 large carrots, cubed

4 medium-size potatoes, cubed

⅓ cup rolled oats or barley

½ cup heavy cream

Danish Green Kale Soup

*I*n a 5-quart soup pot, cook meat, bone, and onion in water until the meat is tender (2 to 3 hours). Remove meat and set aside. Strain stock and chill. Then remove most of the fat.

Place stock in pot. Finely chop or grind the kale and parsley. Add to the stock, along with celery, carrots, potatoes, and rolled oats or barley. Cook 30 minutes. Return some of the meat, finely chopped, to the soup mixture. Cook about 10 to 15 minutes.

Just before serving, add heavy cream to give it a rich, smooth texture. The rest of the beef may be served separately with Danish mustard or any other hot mustard.

Serves 8 to 10

4 cups Poultry Stock (see Index)

¼ teaspoon ginger

½ cup diced cooked chicken

1 cup chopped spinach or
    watercress

2 eggs, well beaten

Egg Drop Soup

*I*n a large soup pot, combine stock, ginger powder, and chicken. Bring to a boil.

Add spinach or watercress. Then pour in the beaten eggs, stirring continuously. Remove immediately and serve.

Serves 4

*F*or making poultry stock, collect leftover poultry bones and freeze them. When you are ready to make the stock, place the frozen bones in the pot with other stock ingredients. They will defrost as you bring the water to a rolling boil. Drain and rinse the bones and other ingredients (and the pot, getting rid of surface scum). Cover all again with cold water, and then start the long cooking process.

Fish Chowder

1 pound fish fillets

2 cups cubed potatoes, well scrubbed but not peeled

2 cups water

⅛ teaspoon pepper

½ cup chopped onions

2 tablespoons butter

2 cups milk

3 tablespoons whole wheat flour

dried basil and/or thyme to taste

*C*ut fillets into 2-inch pieces.

Cook potatoes in water 5 minutes. Add fish and pepper. Simmer, covered, 10 to 12 minutes.

Cook onions in butter until golden and then add to fish mixture.

Add the milk gradually to the flour and then add to chowder. Cook and stir until thickened. Add herbs to taste.

Serves 6

1 medium-size onion, chopped

2 tablespoons butter or oil

2 cups Poultry Stock (see Index)

2 cups water

3 large potatoes, cut in chunks

4 teaspoons dried dillweed

¼ teaspoon pepper

1 pound cod fillets

1 package (9 ounces) frozen, cut
    green beans

½ cup sour cream

2 tablespoons chopped parsley

Fish-Dill Soup

In a large saucepan, saute onion in butter or oil until tender. Add stock, water, potatoes, dillweed, and pepper. Bring to a boil, reduce heat, cover, and simmer 20 minutes.

Meanwhile, cut the fish into 1-inch cubes. Stir into soup along with beans. Return to a boil. Reduce heat and simmer, covered, 10 minutes.

Stir in sour cream. Heat gently but do not boil. Serve sprinkled with parsley.

Serves 6

Golden Chicken Soup

1 4- to 5-pound chicken

3 or 4 beef marrow bones

16 cups water

2 medium-size onions (with a little of the onion skins), 1 studded with 2 whole cloves

1 large carrot, sliced

2 stalks celery, with leaves, chopped

1 bay leaf

2 sprigs dillweed or 1 teaspoon dried

1 parsnip (optional)

1 piece parsley root with tops

2 sprigs parsley

½ teaspoon ginger

3 peppercorns

1 teaspoon kelp powder

2 teaspoons brewer's yeast

2 cloves garlic

juice of 1 lemon

Cut the chicken into halves or quarters. Place the chicken and the bones in a large soup pot. Be sure to include the gizzard and heart. Add water and remaining ingredients. Bring to a boil and simmer until chicken is tender (about 2 hours).

Remove bones, bay leaf, and onion skins. Remove chicken from bones, dice, and return to pot, or, if desired, reserve chicken meat for another use. Skim off excess fat. Serve the soup with either noodles or rice.

Serves 6 to 8

2 tablespoons oil

1½ pounds boneless beef shoulder or chuck, cut into cubes

2 tablespoons whole wheat flour

6 cups water

2 pounds beef soup bones

2 cups chopped tomatoes

3 tablespoons tamari soy sauce

1 tablespoon caraway seeds

1 medium-size onion, coarsely chopped

3 tablespoons chopped parsley

2 large potatoes, diced

2 cups diced cabbage

3 carrots, sliced

3 stalks celery, sliced

Goulash Soup

*I*n a large soup pot, heat oil. Add meat and brown well. Stir in flour and cook 2 minutes.

Add water, bones, tomatoes, tamari, caraway seeds, onion, and parsley. Bring to a boil, cover, reduce heat, and simmer 1 hour. Add remaining ingredients and cook 30 minutes longer, or until meat and vegetables are tender. Remove bones. Serve hot.

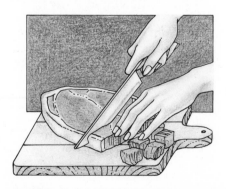

Serves 8 to 10

Hearty Vegetable Soup
with Dumplings

¼ cup olive oil

1 medium-size onion, sliced

1 clove garlic, minced

1 green pepper, coarsely chopped

4 cups Poultry Stock or Beef Stock (see Index)

4 cups tomato juice

2 medium-size zucchini, cut into ¼-inch slices

3 carrots, thinly sliced

1 cup peas, green beans, or cooked dried beans

1 cup corn (2 ears)

1 teaspoon dried basil

¼ teaspoon pepper

Dumplings:

1¼ cups whole wheat flour

3½ teaspoons baking powder

2 tablespoons finely chopped parsley

½ cup milk

freshly grated Romano cheese for garnish

Hearty Vegetable Soup — continued

*H*eat oil in a 5-quart soup pot and saute onion, garlic, and green pepper until soft. Add remaining soup ingredients. Simmer, covered, until vegetables are tender.

In a small bowl, stir together flour, baking powder, and parsley until well blended. Gradually add the milk and stir until just moistened throughout. Drop batter by the tablespoonful into the soup, cover, and simmer 12 minutes without lifting cover. When cooked, dumplings should be puffed and dry inside. Pass grated cheese at the table.

Serves 6 to 8

Lima Bean and Barley Soup

1 pound lima beans

2 pounds beef

16 cups cold water

3 medium-size onions, sliced

pepper to taste

5 carrots, cut in small pieces

3 stalks celery, sliced

3 tablespoons chopped parsley

1 turnip, cubed

½ cup barley

1 cup tomato sauce

Soak lima beans overnight in enough water to cover.

Place meat in a large soup pot. Add water, onions, and pepper to taste. Simmer until meat is about half done (about 1 to 1½ hours). Add drained lima beans, carrots, celery, parsley, turnip, and barley. Continue cooking until the meat is done and the vegetables are soft (about 1 hour). Stir occasionally during cooking period so that the soup will not scorch. Add tomato sauce. Cut beef into small pieces and return to soup pot. Mix well and serve.

Serves 10

2 tablespoons oil

2 cloves garlic, minced or
    pressed

½ cup minced onions

¼ cup diced green peppers

6 tablespoons tomato paste

3 cups liquid (reserve liquid
    from cooked beans and
    add enough water to
    make 3 cups)

¼ teaspoon freshly ground
    black pepper

2 teaspoons dried basil

2 cups cooked chick-peas

1 cup whole wheat elbow
    macaroni

Macaroni and Bean Soup
(Pasta e Fagioli)

*H*eat oil in a large soup pot. Add garlic, onions, and green peppers. Saute 2 to 3 minutes, or until the onions and peppers are tender. Stir in tomato paste and 1 cup of the liquid to thin the tomato paste. Season with black pepper and basil. Add the beans and remaining 2 cups of reserved liquid. When it is simmering again, add the macaroni, stir, and continue cooking until the macaroni is tender (8 to 10 minutes).

Serves 6 to 8

Minestrone

¼ cup safflower oil

1 clove garlic, minced

1 cup chopped onions

1 cup chopped celery

¾ cup tomato paste

10 cups Beef Stock (see Index)

1 cup chopped cabbage

1 cup peas

1 cup diced carrots

¼ teaspoon pepper

½ teaspoon rosemary leaves

2 cups cooked kidney beans

1 cup whole wheat elbow
macaroni

grated Parmesan cheese for
garnish

*H*eat oil and saute garlic, onions, and celery 5 minutes. Stir in tomato paste, stock, cabbage, peas, carrots, pepper, and rosemary. Bring to a boil, cover, and simmer slowly 1 hour.

Add kidney beans and macaroni. Cook 15 minutes longer. Garnish with Parmesan cheese.

Serves 6 to 8

1 3½-pound roasting chicken

12 cups water

3 peppercorns

¼ bay leaf

2 sprigs parsley

4 carrots, sliced

1 stalk celery, with leaves

1 medium-size onion, studded
    with 2 whole cloves

½ cup brown rice

  chopped parsley for garnish

Old-Fashioned Chicken Rice Soup

*R*inse chicken well in cold water. Place in a large soup pot along with water, peppercorns, bay leaf, and parsley. Bring to a boil. Skim any foam from surface.

Reduce heat. Add carrots, celery, and onion with cloves. Cover and simmer 1 hour, or until chicken is tender. Skim off fat.

Lift out chicken and let cool slightly. Remove celery, onion with cloves, and bay leaf and discard. Add rice to stock and simmer slowly until tender.

Meanwhile, remove chicken from bones and cut into bite-size pieces. Return to broth and heat thoroughly (about 20 minutes). Garnish with parsley before serving.

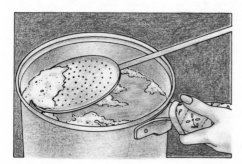

Serves 6 to 8

CREAM SOUPS

Smooth cream soups are an elegant change from the chunky types. They also have the added nutrition of cream or milk, and sometimes cheese or eggs. Many vegetables, as well as poultry and fish, provide a savory base for a velvety smooth cream soup.

The main ingredients of a cream soup may be pureed in a blender or a food processor, giving the soup a silken, even texture. When pureeing in a blender, moisten the contents with some of the cooking liquid before you turn on the motor, and scrape down the sides of the blender each time you blend. Blend in small quantities for best results.

The puree may then be combined with a creamy white sauce, or it may merely be enriched with the addition of milk or cream. Never boil a soup after cream, butter, or eggs have been added, or it may curdle.

As the cook, you will appreciate the simplicity of a puree or cream soup. Relatively few ingredients are needed. Broccoli, fresh peas, spinach, or carrots, flavored with a few herbs or spices, make very appetizing as well as visually appealing cream soups.

A smooth, rich puree with cream lightly incorporated may serve as the prologue to a meal. As a main course served with a slice of whole-grain bread and a salad, it can serve as a complete meal that is both satisfying and nutritious.

4 cups Poultry Stock (see Index)

1 medium-size potato, diced

1 small onion, minced

½ teaspoon tamari soy sauce

½ teaspoon curry powder

3 cups chopped broccoli

1 cup yogurt

2 tablespoons chopped dillweed

1 tablespoon chopped parsley

1 tablespoon chopped chives

Broccoli Bisque

Combine stock, potato, onion, tamari, and curry powder in a saucepan. Cover and simmer 10 minutes, or until tender.

Add broccoli and cook, uncovered, until broccoli is tender (about 5 to 7 minutes).

Puree the mixture with yogurt. Stir in the herbs and serve.

Serves 4

Cream of Asparagus Soup

2 pounds asparagus

3 tablespoons butter

3 tablespoons whole wheat flour

3 cups nonfat milk

*T*rim off only the very end of the asparagus. Cut asparagus into 2-inch pieces and cook in enough boiling water to cover until tender. Do not drain. Place in a blender with cooking water and puree.

Melt butter in a saucepan, then stir in flour to make a *roux.* Gradually add milk and cook, stirring constantly, until slightly thickened.

Add asparagus puree and simmer 5 minutes, stirring occasionally.

Serves 6

1 medium-size onion, diced

3 tablespoons oil

1 pound carrots (5 or 6 large),
    thinly sliced

6 cups Vegetable Stock (see
    Index) or water

1 cup skim milk powder

 white pepper to taste

 chopped dillweed or parsley for
    garnish

Cream of Carrot Soup

Saute onion in oil until transparent. Lift out of the pan and put into a blender.

In the same pan, saute carrots until tender. Set aside a third of the carrots. Put remaining carrots in the blender. Add some of the stock or water and puree. Then heat in the top of a double boiler.

Combine skim milk powder with remaining stock or water, using a wire whisk. Add to the puree. Add pepper to taste.

Add the reserved sauteed carrots to the soup. Garnish with dillweed or parsley.

Serves 6 to 8

Cream of Cauliflower Soup

2 tablespoons butter

1 small onion, coarsely chopped

1 cup Beef Stock or Poultry Stock (see Index)

2 large potatoes, peeled and cut up

1 small head cauliflower (about 1 pound before trimming)

½ cup water

⅛ teaspoon coriander

⅛ teaspoon nutmeg

½ teaspoon white pepper

2 cups half-and-half

chopped chives or watercress

*I*n a large saucepan, melt butter and saute onion until soft. Add stock and potatoes. Cover and cook until potatoes are tender. Do not drain. Puree the mixture in a blender and return it to the saucepan.

Wash and trim the cauliflower and break it into florets. In another saucepan, steam the cauliflower in water until it is barely tender. Do not drain. Remove 1 cup florets with a slotted spoon and reserve them. Puree the rest of the cauliflower with its cooking water, and add it to the potato mixture. Cut the reserved florets into very small pieces, about ½ inch in length, and set aside.

Add coriander, nutmeg, and pepper to the soup and simmer 3 minutes. Stir in half-and-half. Stir in the reserved florets. Heat but do not boil the soup. Garnish each bowl with chopped chives or watercress.

Serves 4 to 6

1½ tablespoons diced onions

3 tablespoons oil

2 tablespoons rye flour

4½ cups Poultry Stock (see Index)

1 tablespoon cornstarch

½ cup water

2¼ cups pumpkin puree

¾ teaspoon ginger

¼ teaspoon nutmeg

1 cup heavy cream

3 egg yolks, slightly beaten

chopped parsley for garnish

Cream of Pumpkin Soup

Saute onions in oil until tender. Stir in flour and cook over low heat, stirring constantly.

Gradually add stock, stirring with a wire whisk until mixture is smooth and boils.

Mix cornstarch with water and add to the mixture, stirring until it begins to thicken and boils again. Add pumpkin puree and spices and transfer to the top of a double boiler.

In a bowl, combine cream, egg yolks, and some of the hot soup. Then add this mixture to the hot soup. Cook just until heated through. Garnish with parsley and serve immediately.

Serves 6 to 8

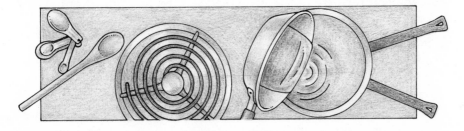

Cream of Spinach Soup

2 pounds fresh spinach, or
  1 10-ounce package frozen

5 cups water

1½ cups skim milk powder

2 tablespoons potato flour or
  brown rice flour

1 cup Beef Stock or Poultry
  Stock (see Index)

grated onion to taste

pepper to taste

Wash spinach and cook in 1 cup water until just tender (about 8 to 10 minutes), stirring occasionally. Process in a blender until coarsely chopped, not pureed.

Make white sauce by combining skim milk powder, flour, stock, and 4 cups water, using a wire whisk. Then cook in a double boiler, over hot water, until sauce is thick.

Add spinach mixture to the white sauce, then add grated onion and pepper to taste. Keep hot in double boiler until ready to serve.

Serves 4 to 6

4 cups coarsely chopped
    potatoes

6 cups Poultry Stock (see
    Index)

3 cups thinly sliced leeks

½ cup skim milk powder

1 cup water

  kelp powder to taste

  tamari soy sauce to taste

1 tablespoon oil

  chopped parsley for garnish

Leek and Potato Soup

Cover potatoes with stock and bring to a boil. Set aside a third of the leeks and add the remainder to the potatoes.

Simmer until potatoes are tender. Put potatoes, leeks, and liquid through a food mill.

Combine skim milk powder and water with a wire whisk. Add to the soup. Season to taste with kelp and tamari.

Saute reserved leeks in oil until tender. Add to the soup just before serving. Garnish with parsley.

Serves 6 to 8

Lettuce Soup

2 large heads iceberg or other lettuce, washed, cored, and leaves pulled apart

2 cups water

4 tablespoons butter

6 scallions, chopped

2 cloves garlic, minced

½ teaspoon white pepper

4 cups hot Poultry Stock (see Index)

2 egg yolks

½ cup heavy cream

3 drops hot pepper sauce

few shreds of cold, crisp lettuce, cut into long ribbons for garnish (optional)

*P*lace separated lettuce leaves in a large soup pot and add water. Cover pot and simmer 15 minutes.

Meanwhile, melt butter in a skillet and add scallions and garlic. Saute until wilted and then add pepper.

In a blender, in several batches, blend lettuce and its liquid with scallions and garlic. Add 3 cups hot stock to the pot. Then add the pureed lettuce mixture.

Beat egg yolks and cream together. Stir 1 ladleful of hot soup into the egg yolk mixture. Remove pot from heat and gradually stir the egg yolk mixture into the soup. Simmer a few minutes, stirring constantly with a wooden spoon. Do not allow to boil. Add hot pepper sauce and serve garnished with lettuce ribbons, if desired.

Serves 6 to 8

2 large leeks

3 stalks celery, sliced

3 tablespoons butter

6 medium-size parsnips, diced

1 cup peas

1 cup wax beans

4 cups Poultry Stock (see Index)

2 cups half-and-half or whole milk

pepper to taste

parsley for garnish

Parsnip Vichyssoise

Saute leeks and celery in butter in a heavy 4-quart soup pot.

Add parsnips, peas, wax beans, and stock and cook in the top of a double boiler until the parsnips are very soft.

Put through a food mill or blender to make a smooth soup. Pour back into the pot and add the half-and-half or milk. Heat until hot, but do not boil.

Add pepper to taste. Garnish with parsley and serve.

Serves 6 to 8

Shrimp Bisque
(Potage Bisque de Crevettes)

1 carrot, sliced

2 scallions or leeks, sliced (use white part of leek)

3 tablespoons butter

1 pound cleaned shrimp

¼ cup brown rice

½ bay leaf

1 teaspoon dried thyme

3 sprigs parsley

black pepper to taste

dash of cayenne pepper

dash of paprika

2 ripe tomatoes, chopped

8 cups water

¾ cup heavy cream

*I*n a 4-quart soup pot, saute carrot and scallions or leeks lightly in butter along with the shrimp. Add the rice, herbs, seasonings, tomatoes, and water. Simmer, uncovered, about 40 minutes.

Shrimp Bisque — continued

Remove bay leaf and parsley, then process in a blender in small batches until smooth, or put through a strainer. Return to pot, add cream, and reheat carefully.

Note: You can make the bisque several hours ahead of time, but add the cream just before reheating to serve.

Serves 10 to 12

Herbs and Spices for the Stockpot

Fresh spices and herbs — parsley, thyme, cloves, and bay leaves — may be used to give stock both fragrance and flavor. If using dried herbs, use about one-third the amount you would use if they were fresh. Herbs and spices yield their flavors readily to the cooking liquid, so they should not be added before the last 45 minutes to an hour of cooking. To ensure easy retrieval, gather the spices and herbs into a cheesecloth bag or pouch *(bouquet garni)* before adding them. If whole, large leaves or seeds are being used, tie them to a stalk of celery or a leek. Smaller fragments may be tied into a piece of cheesecloth and anchored down beneath a soup bone.

Potato Soup

3 medium-size potatoes, diced

1 medium-size onion, chopped

1 cup diced celery

2 cups water or Vegetable Stock
(see Index)

2 tablespoons chopped parsley

2 cups milk

⅛ teaspoon white pepper

⅛ teaspoon nutmeg

2 teaspoons chopped dillweed
or 1 teaspoon dried

*I*n a large saucepan, combine potatoes, onion, celery, and water or stock. Cover the saucepan and cook over medium heat about 20 minutes.

Place about half the potatoes and onion with the potato water in a blender and puree, making sure the blender is not more than half full. You can use a food processor instead of a blender, or you can mash the ingredients with a wooden spoon or potato masher.

Return the mixture to the pot and add milk, pepper, nutmeg, and dillweed. Heat and stir until soup is pleasantly hot, but do not boil.

Serves 4 to 6

2 small onions, thinly sliced

2 tablespoons oil

broccoli trimmings (stems, leaves, and leftover buds)

2 carrots, grated

tops of 4 stalks celery

1 bay leaf

¼ teaspoon pepper

5 to 6 cups cold water

2 to 3 cups yogurt

Summer Soup

Saute onions in oil until transparent. Add broccoli trimmings and any other leftover vegetables and vegetable trimmings on hand. Cook 1 minute.

Add all remaining ingredients except yogurt, bring to a boil, cover, reduce heat, and simmer gently 1 hour. (The amount of water you will need depends on your supply of vegetable trimmings—use just enough water to cover the vegetables in the pot.)

When cooked, puree the soup in a blender until almost smooth. At serving time, warm the soup slightly and stir in yogurt, allowing ½ cup of yogurt per cup of soup.

Note: This cool, creamy soup is a great way to use up garden leftovers on a hot day. For cooler days, add cooked grains and serve the soup hot, as is, or with strands of egg, in the manner of Chinese egg drop soup.

Serves 6 to 8

Watercress Cream Soup

1 large bunch watercress

2 tablespoons whole wheat flour

6 cups milk

3 tablespoons minced onion

1 teaspoon chopped basil

Wash watercress and pat dry. Saving 6 sprigs for garnish, finely chop the remaining cress and set aside.

Make a paste of the flour and ¼ cup of the milk in a large saucepan. Slowly stir in remaining milk, onion, and basil. Cook, stirring constantly, until mixture comes to a boil. It should thicken slightly.

Stir in chopped watercress and simmer only 3 minutes. Serve immediately. Garnish each serving with a sprig of watercress.

Serves 6

¼ cup butter

1 medium-size onion, chopped

6 scallions and tops, thinly
    sliced

¾ pound mushrooms, sliced

2 teaspoons paprika

¼ cup whole wheat flour

6 cups Poultry Stock (see
    Index)

2 egg yolks

1½ cups yogurt

¼ teaspoon dried dillweed

Yogurt Mushroom Soup

*I*n a 3-quart saucepan, melt butter over medium-high heat. Add the onion and scallions and cook, stirring occasionally, until limp. Add mushrooms and cook, stirring occasionally, until mushrooms are soft. Stir in paprika and flour. Then gradually stir in stock. Cook, while stirring, until thickened. Cover and simmer 30 minutes.

Lightly beat together egg yolks. Mix with yogurt and dillweed. Stir about 1 cup of the hot soup into the egg mixture. Return to soup and cook, while stirring, over low heat just until thickened. Do not allow it to boil.

Serves 6 to 8

CHILLED SOUPS

*A*lthough chilled soups seem like a novel way of enjoying soup, they are not really new. They first appeared in the French court of Louis XIV; vichyssoise, a classic pureed soup of leek and potato, has been a gourmet treat since the turn of this century. A cold soup such as this can be a perfect refreshment on a warm day. Either pureed vegetables or fruits can serve as a delicious basis for chilled soups. The preparation is elementary; sometimes it involves no cooking at all.

Gazpacho, a raw-vegetable soup popular in Latin America, is a colorful blend of chopped vegetables that may be pureed to different consistencies. Gazpacho makes a refreshing, healthful cocktail. Garnished with a dollop of sour cream or yogurt, it provides even more nourishment. This popular, very flamboyant, chilled soup requires no cooking.

Fruits make especially delicious chilled soups. They combine winning sensations of sweet and tart. Many fruit soups may have their sweetness heightened or rounded off with a contrasting garnish. In making fruit soups, the fruit may be raw or partly cooked.

Try beginning a meal with a chilled fruit or vegetable soup to whet the appetite. Some of these soups make a satisfying between-meals treat or a meal-in-a-glass breakfast or lunch for people too busy for more time-consuming meals. The soups are rich in the vitamins and nutrients that fresh vegetables and fruits offer, yet those without milk or cream are low in calories.

2 avocados, peeled and cut
in chunks

2 tablespoons lemon juice

2½ cups Poultry Stock or
Vegetable Stock (see Index)

1 tablespoon butter

1 medium-size onion, diced

1 tablespoon whole wheat
flour

1½ cups yogurt

3 tomatoes, cut in bite-size
chunks

⅛ teaspoon cayenne pepper

⅛ teaspoon black pepper

chopped dillweed or parsley

Avocado Tomato Soup

*I*n a blender or food processor, combine avocados, lemon juice, and ½ cup stock. Process until smooth. Pour mixture into a large bowl.

In a 3-quart saucepan, melt the butter, add the onion, and cook until wilted. Sprinkle with flour and stir. Add remaining stock, stirring briskly with a wire whisk. When mixture is well blended, remove from heat. Add to the avocado mixture.

Add the yogurt, tomatoes, cayenne, and black pepper. Chill. Garnish with dillweed or parsley.

Serves 4 to 6

1 quart blackberries or
    1 1¼-pound package frozen
    unsweetened blackberries

2¼ cups water

4 lemon slices

6 tablespoons honey

Blackberry Soup

2½ tablespoons cornstarch

¼ teaspoon cinnamon

⅛ teaspoon cloves

sour cream or yogurt for
    garnish

*R*eserve 1 cup blackberries. Combine remaining berries with 2 cups water, lemon, and honey. Simmer 5 minutes, mashing berries to extract all the juice. Strain, pressing the pulp to remove juice. There should be about 3 cups of juice.

Reheat juice, dissolve cornstarch in ¼ cup water, and stir into boiling juice. Lower heat and cook until thickened. Cool. Add reserved berries and spices. Chill completely and serve with a dollop of sour cream or yogurt.

 Serves 4 to 6

2 tablespoons butter

1 cup finely chopped onions

⅓ cup barley

3 cups water

3 cups yogurt

1 cup milk

small handful of finely
    chopped mint

Chilled Barley Bisque

*I*n a heavy soup pot, melt butter and saute onions until wilted. Add barley and water and simmer until barley is very tender (about 1½ hours).

Cool and refrigerate the soup. Just before serving, stir in the yogurt, milk, and chopped mint, reserving a few tablespoons to sprinkle on top. Serve in glass bowls.

Serves 6 to 8

Cold Melon Soup

1 large, ripe cantaloupe

¼ teaspoon cinnamon
   (optional)

2½ cups orange juice

3 tablespoons lime juice

fresh mint sprigs for garnish

*R*emove seeds from melon and cut the pulp into cubes.

Place pulp, cinnamon, and ½ cup orange juice in a blender and puree.

Combine remaining 2 cups orange juice and lime juice and stir into the puree. Pour mixture into a bowl, cover, and refrigerate at least 1 hour before serving.

Remove soup from the refrigerator; stir mixture and pour into a soup tureen or individual soup bowls. Serve garnished with sprigs of fresh mint.

Serves 4 to 6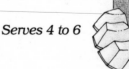

3 cucumbers

1 tablespoon chopped dillweed

1 tablespoon chopped parsley

1 large clove garlic, minced

1 cup buttermilk or yogurt (or half sour cream and half yogurt)

chopped dillweed for garnish

Cool Cucumber Buttermilk Bisque

*P*eel and halve cucumbers and remove the seeds. Chop cucumbers very fine with a sharp knife.

Combine cucumbers with remaining ingredients. If a finer consistency is desired, ingredients can be processed in a blender. Cover and chill. Serve in clear glass bowls with ice cubes, garnished with fresh dillweed.

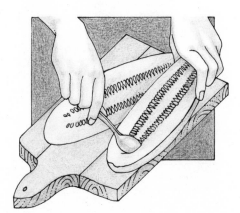

Serves 4

Creamy Avocado Soup

2 ripe avocados, peeled and cubed

1½ cups water

2 teaspoons powdered vegetable concentrate

1 scallion, sliced

1½ cups yogurt

2 tablespoons lemon juice

dash of hot pepper sauce

2 tomatoes, peeled and cubed

Garnish

yogurt

chopped scallions

Combine avocados, water, vegetable concentrate, scallions, yogurt, lemon juice, and hot pepper sauce in a blender. Process until smooth.

Add tomatoes and chill. Serve topped with yogurt and chopped scallions.

Serves 6 to 8

4 medium-size peaches, cut
    into chunks

1 cup yogurt

¼ teaspoon cinnamon

  pinch of ginger

  pinch of curry powder

Garnish

  mint leaves (optional)

  strawberries (optional)

Easy
Peach Soup

*P*uree peaches in a blender until smooth. Add yogurt, cinnamon, ginger, and curry, blending just enough to mix. Pour into individual bowls and serve immediately. Garnish with mint leaves and strawberries if desired.

Serves 4

Gazpacho

3 cups ripe cored, peeled, seeded
    and chopped tomatoes
    (about 6 tomatoes)

½ cup finely chopped onions

1 cucumber, peeled and diced

½ cup finely chopped green
    peppers

1 small clove garlic, minced

3 tablespoons chopped parsley

2 tablespoons chopped chives

2 cups tomato juice

⅓ cup red wine vinegar

¼ cup olive oil

¼ teaspoon cayenne pepper

thin slices of cucumber for
    garnish

*I*n a large bowl, combine tomatoes, onions, cucumber, green peppers, garlic, parsley, and chives. Add tomato juice, wine vinegar, olive oil, and cayenne and mix together.

Cover bowl and place in the refrigerator at least 2 hours to blend flavors.

Serve soup ice cold, garnished with thin slices of cucumber.

Serves 4 to 6

Note: To loosen the tomato skins for peeling, insert fork into tomatoes and plunge into boiling water for a few seconds. Skins may then be easily slipped off. To seed, cut tomatoes in half and scoop seeds out with a small spoon.

1 tablespoon tapioca granules

½ cup water

4 cups orange juice

1 large or 2 small bananas, diced

1 orange, seeded and diced

1 juicy ripe peach, diced

shredded coconut

Orange Fruit Soup

*I*n a large soup pot, combine the tapioca and water. Bring to a boil, stirring frequently, and cook until tapioca is transparent.

Add the orange juice and heat. Then add the rest of the ingredients. Stir until heated through (just a few seconds). Ladle into bowls, sprinkle with coconut, and serve.

Serves 6 to 8

Plum Soup

2 cups plums, pitted and cut into eighths

¼ cup honey

½ teaspoon cinnamon

¼ lemon, sliced very thin

2½ cups water

1 tablespoon tapioca granules

1 egg, beaten

*I*n a medium-size saucepan, combine plums, honey, cinnamon, lemon, and 2 cups water and simmer, covered, 15 minutes, or until plums are soft.

In another medium-size saucepan, combine tapioca and ½ cup water and bring to a boil, stirring frequently until tapioca is transparent. Add this to the plum mixture and bring it to a boil, stirring occasionally.

Remove from heat and add a little of the hot soup to the beaten egg, stirring to blend. Stir this back into the soup and blend well. Serve warm or cold.

Serves 4 to 6

1 can salmon (7¾ ounces)

4 small cucumbers

1 medium-size onion, chopped

1 cup Poultry Stock, Vegetable Stock, or Fish Stock (see Index)

2 tablespoons lemon juice

½ teaspoon white pepper

1 teaspoon chopped dillweed or ½ teaspoon dried

1 cup yogurt

Garnish

toasted sesame seeds

paprika

Salmon-Cucumber Soup

*F*lake the salmon in its liquid. Peel the cucumbers if they have been waxed and cut them in chunks. Place salmon with its liquid, cucumbers, and onion in a blender or food processor and process until smooth.

Add stock, lemon juice, pepper, and dillweed. Blend thoroughly. Stir in the yogurt and chill.

Serve in chilled bowls garnished with sesame seeds and paprika.

Serves 4

Strawberry Soup

3 pints (approximately) fresh
strawberries or
1½ packages frozen
strawberries (30 ounces)

5 tablespoons honey

2½ tablespoons cornstarch

½ cup orange juice

½ cup sour cream or yogurt

Wash and slice enough fresh strawberries to make 3¾ cups. Add 3 tablespoons honey and stir well to coat the berries evenly. Set aside for an hour or so. If using frozen strawberries, slice them, drizzle 3 tablespoons honey over them, stir well, and thaw completely.

Drain berries. You should have about 1½ cups strawberry juice and 2¼ cups berries. Put juice into a blender and add half of the berries, processing to make a very liquid puree. Heat puree to the boiling point.

Dissolve cornstarch in orange juice and stir into boiling strawberry puree. Cook a minute or two, or until mixture is clear and thickened. Cool slightly and add 2 tablespoons honey and remaining strawberries.

Chill completely and serve garnished with a dollop of sour cream or yogurt. Or, if desired, add sour cream or yogurt to the soup, stirring a little of the soup into the sour cream or yogurt first, to thin it, and then stirring it into the rest of the soup. Chill completely before serving.

Serves 4 to 6

½ cup raisins

¼ cup lemon juice

1 stick cinnamon (about
    2-inch length)

6 thin navel orange slices

5 thin lemon slices

3¼ cups water

2 cups pitted, dark, sweet
    cherries (fresh or frozen)

2 cups peeled and sliced
    peaches

⅓ cup honey

2 tablespoons cornstarch

  yogurt for garnish

Swiss Cherry Soup

*I*n a medium-size saucepan, combine raisins, lemon juice, cinnamon, and orange and lemon slices. Add 3 cups water. Place over medium heat and bring to a boil. Reduce heat, cover, and simmer 15 minutes. Remove cinnamon stick.

Add cherries, peaches, and honey to soup mixture. Bring to a boil.

Meanwhile, blend cornstarch with ¼ cup water and then slowly add to the hot fruit mixture. Cook, stirring, until soup is clear (about 2 to 3 minutes).

Remove saucepan from heat and immediately pour hot soup into a bowl and cool. Place soup in refrigerator, covered, several hours or overnight before serving.

Serve soup chilled and garnished with a dollop of yogurt.

Serves 6 to 8

Zucchini Soup

4 tablespoons butter

6 scallions, chopped

5 medium-size zucchini (about 1½ to 2 pounds), sliced ½ inch thick

2½ cups Poultry Stock (see Index)

1 bunch watercress, leaves only (reserve a few whole sprigs for garnish)

2 cups yogurt

pepper to taste

*M*elt butter in a large skillet and saute scallions 2 minutes. Add zucchini, stir, and saute 3 minutes more. Stir in stock, cover, and simmer 15 minutes longer.

Add watercress leaves and cook until wilted (about 1 minute). Remove from heat and cool.

Puree in several batches in a blender. Chill until ice cold. Before serving, stir in yogurt with a wire whisk and add pepper. Garnish each bowl with a sprig of watercress.

Serves 4 to 6

VEGETABLE
SOUPS

*E*veryone should eat fresh vegetables every day for their ability to aid many vital bodily processes. They have a healing and invigorating power not to be underestimated. Putting them in a good tasty soup is an excellent way to get your vegetables. If you prepare them in other ways, even brief boiling in water causes important minerals and vitamins to slip into the liquid. When that liquid is a soup, you know you are getting as much goodness as possible from vegetables.

The color of the vegetable is a clue to the type of nutrition it contains. The darker the green leafy vegetable, the more vitamins, especially vitamins A, C, E, K, and a number of B's and minerals, especially iron, copper, magnesium, and calcium, it has. Similarly for yellows and oranges, the stronger and deeper the colors, the more vitamins, especially A. For a soup with added vitamin A, add extra carrots, kale, parsley, and dandelion greens.

If you want extra C, parsley and turnip greens are on top of the list, followed by dark green, shiny peppers.

Dandelion and mustard greens are good sources of calcium, as are parsley, kale, and turnip greens. Beets, Swiss chard, dandelion, parsley, and spinach are excellent sources of iron.

With this wide variety of fresh and nutritious vegetables available, you can orchestrate a vegetable soup that can not help but be wholesome and tasty.

Chicken Corn Soup

8 cups water

4 chicken wings and 4 thighs
   (2¼ pounds parts)

½ cup chopped onions

1 cup chopped celery

2 tablespoons oil

1 cup chopped potatoes

4 cups frozen corn

2 teaspoons tamari soy sauce

Combine water and chicken parts in a 4-quart soup pot. Cook until chicken is tender (about 1 hour). Strain. Remove chicken from bones and put back into stock.

Saute onions and celery in oil until onions are golden. Add to soup with potatoes, corn, and tamari. Cook until vegetables are tender (about 30 to 40 minutes).

Serves 6 to 8

Quenelles:

½ pound raw ground chicken

⅓ cup heavy cream

3 eggs

½ teaspoon white pepper

 pinch each of mace, cloves, nutmeg, and thyme

Consomme:

1 cup peas, cooked

16 asparagus tips, cooked

8 cups hot Poultry Stock (see Index)

32 *quenelles*

2 or 3 scallions, chopped

Consomme Danoise *with Chicken* Quenelles

Combine chicken, cream, eggs, and seasonings in a blender and puree until smooth. Refrigerate at least 1 hour.

Fill a large saucepan three-quarters full of water and bring to a boil. Reduce heat to simmer. Wet 2 teaspoons in the hot water, scoop out a spoonful of chicken mixture, and use the other spoon to make a neat, egg-shaped dumpling. Wet spoons before shaping each dumpling. Drop the *quenelles* into the simmering water and cook 3 to 5 minutes. Leave them in the water but remove the pan from direct heat and keep water warm. Serve within 30 minutes.

Add peas and asparagus tips to heated stock and simmer 10 minutes. Add dumplings and scallions and serve.

Serves 4 to 6

Escarole Soup

¼ small chicken (breast quarter or leg quarter)

10 cups water

1 medium-size onion, chopped

1 stalk celery, chopped

pepper to taste

1 head fresh escarole, cut into 1-inch pieces

1 egg, beaten

2 tablespoons grated Parmesan or Romano cheese

*I*n a large saucepan, combine chicken, water, onion, celery, and pepper. Cook until chicken is tender (about 30 minutes). Remove chicken and take meat from bones, tearing into small pieces. Return chicken pieces to stock.

Cook escarole in a small amount of water until just tender (about 5 minutes). Drain and add to stock.

Before serving, mix beaten egg and cheese. Stir briskly into the boiling soup.

Serves 6 to 8

2½ cups thinly sliced onions

4 tablespoons oil

6 cups Beef Stock (see Index)

pepper to taste

cumin to taste (optional)

Parmesan cheese for garnish

French Onion Soup

*I*n a heavy-bottom soup pot, brown onions in oil until golden brown. Add stock and simmer, tightly covered, about 1 hour.

Season with pepper and cumin to taste. Sprinkle Parmesan cheese over the top or serve it separately.

Serves 4 to 6

Garden Soup

1 bunch scallions (about 6)

1¼ pounds frozen peas

2 cups Poultry Stock (see Index)

white pepper to taste

½ large head romaine lettuce, coarsely chopped

¼ pound spinach, coarsely chopped

2 cups light cream

*T*hinly slice scallions. Set aside a third of them for garnish. Add the rest to frozen peas, bring to a boil in stock, and add pepper. Reduce heat and simmer about 10 minutes, or until peas are nearly tender.

Add lettuce and spinach, reserving 8 or 10 leaves of spinach, thinly sliced for garnish. Simmer about 5 minutes, stirring to cook the greens evenly, until lettuce is tender, but the rib of the leaves still crunchy. Process mixture in a blender to a smooth puree. Stir in cream. Refrigerate several hours. Garnish with reserved sliced spinach and scallions.

Serves 6

½ pound beef flank or shin

1½ pounds beef bones

4 cups water

1 head cabbage (1½ to
2 pounds), shredded

1 large onion, diced

3 tablespoons butter

4 cups chopped, cooked
tomatoes

2 pitted prunes, chopped

2 tablespoons raisins

1½ tablespoons lemon juice

1 tablespoon honey

Russian Cabbage Soup

*I*n a 4-quart soup pot, cook meat and bones in water 30 minutes. Skim off any foam that accumulates on top.

In a large skillet, saute the cabbage and onion in butter 3 minutes. Add tomatoes and cook until the cabbage is limp. Add the cabbage-tomato mixture to the stock.

Add the remaining ingredients. Bring the soup to a boil and then simmer 1½ hours, or until the meat is tender. Remove the meat from the pot, cut into cubes, and return to the pot.

Serves 8

Sorrel Soup

1 pound beef short ribs

8 cups water

1 carrot, chopped

1 large potato, diced

1 large onion, chopped

½ teaspoon chopped basil

pepper to taste

3 cups sorrel

2 hard-cooked eggs, finely chopped

2 tablespoons chopped parsley

sour cream for garnish

Combine beef and water in a 5-quart soup pot, bring to a boil, reduce heat, and simmer 1½ hours.

Add carrot, potato, onion, and basil and cook 20 minutes longer. Add pepper to taste.

Meanwhile, cook sorrel in a minimum of water about 5 minutes. Puree in a blender and then add to the soup.

Add eggs and parsley and heat briefly. Serve with sour cream.

Serves 8

Note: This exceptionally delicious soup can be made with spinach or beet greens instead of sorrel.

1 medium-size onion, finely
   minced

1 small clove garlic, minced

3 tablespoons olive or corn oil

¼ cup tomato puree

¼ cup water

2 cups cooked navy or kidney
   beans

3 cups Vegetable Stock (see
   Index) or water

1 carrot, diced

½ cup celery leaves, chopped

2 cups Swiss chard, shredded

   dash of pepper

¼ teaspoon dried basil

1 teaspoon dried oregano or
   marjoram

   chopped parsley for garnish

Swiss Chard Soup with Beans

In a saucepan, saute onion and garlic in oil until lightly browned. Add tomato puree and water, and let this basic sauce simmer about 15 minutes, or until it has cooked down.

Add beans, stock or water, carrot, celery leaves, Swiss chard, and seasonings. Cover and cook over medium heat until vegetables are soft.

Liquefy soup in a blender. You will have a thick, creamy soup that can be thinned, if desired. Garnish with chopped parsley.

Serves 4

Note: For a hearty supper dish, try this soup thinned down, with brown rice or egg noodles cooked in it.

Tomato Bouillon

4 cups tomato juice

1 bay leaf

1 small onion, studded with
2 whole cloves

1 stalk celery, with leaves

3 peppercorns

4 cups Poultry Stock or Beef
Stock (see Index)

1 tablespoon honey (optional)

Garnish

chopped parsley

yogurt

*I*n a large soup pot, combine tomato juice, bay leaf, onion with cloves, celery, and peppercorns and slowly bring to a boil. Reduce heat and simmer 30 minutes.

Remove from heat and strain. Add stock and honey if desired, place over medium heat, and simmer 15 minutes longer.

Serve garnished with chopped parsley and a dollop of yogurt.

Serves 6 to 8

2 medium-size onions, diced

2 leeks, thinly sliced (if leeks are not available, use more onions)

1 clove garlic, minced

¼ cup olive oil

2 tablespoons chopped parsley

1 teaspoon crushed thyme

1 bay leaf

2 cups peeled and diced tomatoes

3 cups Poultry Stock or Beef Stock (see Index)

tamari soy sauce to taste

1 to 2 teaspoons honey

Garnish

chopped parsley

chopped scallion tops

Tomato, Leek, and Onion Soup

Saute onions, leeks, and garlic in olive oil until transparent but not brown.

Combine sauteed vegetables, parsley, thyme, bay leaf, tomatoes, and stock in a 2-quart saucepan. Simmer over medium heat until tomatoes are cooked and flavors are well combined. Remove bay leaf.

Season with tamari and honey to taste. Garnish with chopped parsley and scallion tops.

Serves 4 to 6

Vegetable Garlic Soup

1 cup lentils

4 cups water

4 cloves garlic, minced

1 cup chopped onions

¼ cup chopped parsley

1 cup chopped celery

3 cups chopped tomatoes

¼ teaspoon cayenne pepper

½ teaspoon dry mustard

1 cup mashed potatoes (3 potatoes) or ½ cup oatmeal

In a 4-quart soup pot, cook lentils in water until tender (about 45 minutes). Add more water so there are about 4 cups of liquid in the pot.

Add remaining ingredients except mashed potatoes or oatmeal and simmer until tender.

Add mashed potatoes or oatmeal and stir until soup is thickened.

Serves 8 to 10

2 to 3 tablespoons butter or oil

3 medium-size onions, chopped

4 medium-size potatoes, diced

4 carrots, thinly sliced

2 turnips, diced

¼ head cabbage, shredded or chopped

4 cups tomato juice

1 cup chopped parsley or chives

Vegetarian Vegetable Soup

*H*eat butter or oil in a large soup pot and saute onions until tender. Add the vegetables, along with enough water to cover. Simmer the mixture until the potatoes and turnips are tender (about 30 minutes).

Add tomato juice and continue cooking until it is heated through. Add the chopped parsley or chives and serve.

Serves 6 to 8

Note: To make a creamy vegetable soup, saute the onions as directed above. Cook the remaining vegetables in enough water to cover and puree with the cooking water (half at a time) in a blender. Add the mixture to the onions. Cook 30 minutes. Add tomato juice and continue cooking until it is heated through. Season with a dash of tamari soy sauce, and sprinkle with parsley just before serving.

Winter Squash Soup

1 medium-size onion, chopped

3 tablespoons butter

1 tomato, peeled, seeded, and chopped

1 to 2 teaspoons seeded and chopped hot red pepper, or cayenne pepper to taste

1 clove garlic, minced

2 pounds winter squash, peeled, seeded, and cut into ½-inch cubes (about 4 cups)

4 cups Beef Stock (see Index)

½ teaspoon cumin

½ teaspoon coriander

black pepper to taste

chopped parsley for garnish

*I*n a large saucepan, saute onion in butter for a few minutes. Add tomato, hot red pepper or cayenne, and garlic and saute 5 minutes longer. Then add squash, stock, and seasonings. Bring mixture to a boil and simmer, covered, about 20 minutes, or until squash is very tender. When ready to serve, garnish with parsley.

Serves 4 to 6

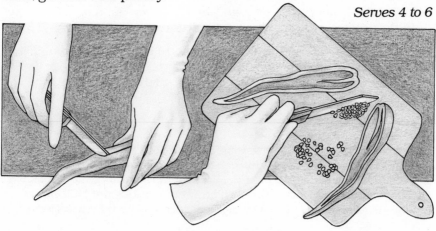

GRAIN
AND LEGUME
SOUPS

*T*he same rich variety of textures and flavors that grains and legumes provide for other types of meals can be translated into dozens of good-tasting soups. Grains and beans, in fact, seem to have a natural affinity for soups. They contribute a natural body and thickening power.

In terms of good health, soups made with the various grains and dried beans are unmatched. If you wish to replace some of the meat in your diet with a protein source lower in fat and cholesterol, this is a perfectly delicious way to do it. Both grains and legumes contain significant amounts of amino acids, as well as complex carbohydrates, important vitamins, and minerals. Soups that combine both grains and legumes are especially nutritious because protein patterns of these foods complement each other. Split peas and barley, a classic combination, are a perfect example of this.

No matter which of the good whole grains you choose for soups—bulgur, rice, oats, or rye, to name a few—you are sure to find their individual nutty flavors pleasing. Dried beans, peas, and lentils present a whole range of tastes that mingle well with meat stocks and fresh vegetables in a good hearty soup.

Grain and legume soups are good choices as the centerpiece of a full, rounded meal that is filling, tasty, and nourishing.

Caribbean Banana Soup

½ cup brown rice

6 ripe bananas, coarsely mashed (about 1½ cups)

4 cups Beef Stock (see Index)

½ cup minced onions

¼ cup diced green peppers

2 cloves garlic, minced

2 tablespoons oil

¼ cup freshly grated or dried coconut

¼ cup ground peanuts

cayenne pepper to taste

Cook brown rice according to preferred method.

Combine bananas and stock in a saucepan and simmer 10 minutes, stirring occasionally.

Saute onions, green peppers, and garlic in oil for a few minutes. Add coconut and saute until it is golden brown, stirring constantly. Add sauteed mixture to banana soup, then the peanuts and rice. Season with cayenne to taste. Simmer, covered, about 15 minutes. Serve hot.

Serves 6 to 8

1½ cups chick-peas

2 cloves garlic, minced

1 slice whole-grain bread,
      diced in ¾-inch pieces

2 tablespoons oil

2 tablespoons chopped parsley

1 large potato, peeled and
      diced

1 large tomato, chopped

1 bay leaf

½ head cabbage, shredded
      (about 4 cups)

6 cups combined bean liquid
      and water

½ pound spinach, chopped

Chick-Pea and Cabbage Soup

Cook chick-peas according to preferred method. Drain and reserve liquid.

Saute garlic and bread in oil until garlic begins to deepen in color. Remove pan from heat and stir in parsley. Combine mixture with potato, cooked chick-peas, tomato, bay leaf, cabbage, and bean liquid and water in a large pot and cook until potato is done (about 15 to 20 minutes). The bread will soften and thicken the soup.

About 5 minutes before serving, add spinach and continue cooking until it is done but still keeps its bright green color. Serve hot.

Serves 6 to 8

Chili Bean and Rice Soup

1 pound pink, red, or pinto beans

6 to 8 cups boiling water

2 cloves garlic, crushed

1 medium-size onion, diced

1 bay leaf

¼ teaspoon dried thyme

¼ teaspoon dried marjoram

½ cup brown rice

1½ cups Beef Stock, Chicken Stock, or Vegetable Stock (see Index)

2 cups stewed tomatoes

1 teaspoon chili powder

¼ teaspoon cayenne pepper

Wash the beans and soak them in enough water to cover for 1 hour. Drain and put them in a large soup pot. Add boiling water, garlic, onion, bay leaf, thyme, and marjoram. Cover and simmer 1½ hours. Don't let the beans boil dry. Add hot water as needed. Add the brown rice, stock,

Chili Bean and Rice Soup — continued

tomatoes, and seasonings. Continue to cook another hour. When the beans are tender, mash half of them (about 3 cups) with some liquid. You can serve the rest of the beans in the soup or reserve them for another use.

Serves 6 to 8

*B*eans and brown rice both contain excellent body-building nutrients. Beans are a little short of the amino acid methionine, a deficiency that is made up by the brown rice. Together they provide a complete protein equivalent to what you get in meat. Many beans are rich in iron, phosphorus, and potassium.

1 pound dried beans (white beans, pinto beans, broad beans, soybeans, or chickpeas)

4 tablespoons oil

Creamed White Bean Soup

1 medium-size onion, sliced

1 large carrot, sliced

1 large stalk celery, sliced

1 teaspoon tamari soy sauce

2 cups milk

2 egg yolks

½ cup heavy cream or sour cream

*P*ick over and soak the beans for 8 hours or overnight. In a deep heavy soup pot, combine beans and soaking water, oil, onion, carrot, celery, and tamari. Cover with additional water, if necessary, to a level of 1 inch above the beans. Bring to a boil slowly, reduce to a simmer, and cover the pot. Cook until beans become very soft. Puree the whole mixture.

Return puree to the pot, add milk, and adjust the seasoning. In a small bowl, mix the egg yolks and cream. Stir about ½ cup of the hot soup into the yolk mixture, then stir the yolk mixture into the soup in the pot. Warm the soup over very low heat. Do not allow it to boil, or the egg will separate.

Serves 6 to 8

6 cups Poultry Stock (see Index)

½ cup brown rice

1 egg

2 egg yolks

¼ cup lemon juice

2 tablespoons snipped parsley

⅛ teaspoon cayenne pepper

chopped dillweed for garnish

Greek Lemon Soup (Avgalemono)

*P*lace stock in a heavy 4-quart soup pot and bring to a boil. Add brown rice and cook until tender (30 to 35 minutes).

Put whole egg and 2 egg yolks into a medium-size bowl and beat with a rotary beater or wire whisk until light and frothy. Slowly add the lemon juice, beating together thoroughly.

Just before serving, dilute the egg-lemon mixture with 1 cup hot stock, beating constantly with wire whisk until well blended. Gradually add the diluted mixture to the remaining hot soup, stirring constantly. Bring almost to the boiling point—*do not boil, or the soup will curdle.* Stir in the parsley and cayenne.

Remove from heat and serve immediately, garnished with dillweed.

Serves 6 to 8

Pistachio and Lentil Soup

3 medium-size onions, chopped

2 tablespoons butter

2 carrots, chopped

2 stalks celery, with leaves, chopped

2 cups lentils

6 cups Vegetable Stock (see Index)

freshly ground pepper to taste

pinch each of ginger, curry, and thyme

1 cup chopped pistachios

Garnish

paprika

chopped coriander or parsley

In a 5-quart soup pot, saute onions in butter. Add carrots and celery and cook 5 minutes without browning. Add lentils and stock and simmer gently until the lentils are cooked (about 40 minutes).

Puree the mixture in a blender or a food mill. Add seasonings. Then stir in the pistachios, heat through, and serve with paprika and coriander or parsley sprinkled over the top.

Serves 8

1 pound lentils

2 carrots, chopped

3 stalks celery, sliced, or ½ cup
      cubed celeriac

8 cups water

1 medium-size onion, chopped

1 teaspoon oil

8 cups chopped, cooked tomatoes

Lentil Soup

In a 5-quart soup pot, cook lentils, carrots, and celery or celeriac in water, covered, until tender (about 40 minutes). Add more water if necessary.

Saute onion in oil and add to cooked lentil mixture. Stir in tomatoes and simmer 10 to 15 minutes longer.

Serve hot with whole wheat bread.

Serves 16

Peanut Butter Soup

1 medium-size onion, chopped

1 cup chopped celery

2 tablespoons oil

¼ cup peanut butter

2½ cups Poultry Stock (see Index)

1 cup tomato juice

⅛ teaspoon white pepper

½ teaspoon coriander

1 cup yogurt

Saute onion and celery in oil until tender. Stir peanut butter into sauteed mixture. Add stock, tomato juice, and seasonings. Bring to a boil and simmer about 10 minutes.

Just before serving, stir in yogurt. Heat but do not boil. Serve hot.

Serves 4 to 6

1 cup pinto beans

3 cups water

2 cups tomato juice

1 parsnip, chopped

1 medium-size onion, chopped

1 carrot, chopped

¼ teaspoon dried sage

   pepper to taste

Pinto-Vegetable Soup

Soak beans in enough water to cover 4 to 6 hours.

Drain and then place them in a large soup pot. Add water and cook 1 hour.

Add remaining ingredients and continue to cook 30 minutes more. Serve piping hot.

Serves 4

Rosemary-Egg Noodle Soup

6 cups Poultry Stock (see Index)

¼ cup barley

1 cup chopped scallions

1½ cups snap beans, cut in 1-inch pieces

1 cup grated carrots

2 teaspoons dried rosemary

2 teaspoons chopped celery leaves

1 cup whole wheat egg noodles

*I*n a heavy 4-quart soup pot, bring stock to a boil. Add barley and simmer 25 minutes.

Stir in scallions, snap beans, carrots, rosemary, and celery leaves and simmer 20 minutes. Add egg noodles and cook until done (12 to 15 minutes).

Serves 6 to 8

8 cups water

1 large onion, thinly sliced

5 cloves garlic, sliced

1 large leek, finely sliced

3 medium-size carrots, sliced

3 large potatoes, cubed

2 cups cooked navy beans

 bouquet garni

1 cup whole wheat elbow
 macaroni

1½ cups cut green beans

2 small zucchini, sliced

1 pattypan squash, cubed

 pinch of cayenne pepper

⅓ cup packed basil leaves

1 cup grated Parmesan cheese

1 tomato, peeled and chopped

¾ cup olive oil

Soupe au Pistou

*B*oil water in a large soup pot. Add onion, 1 clove garlic, leek, carrots, potatoes, beans, and *bouquet garni.* Cover and simmer 30 minutes, or until the beans are very soft but still hold their shape. Add macaroni and cook 5 minutes, then add green beans, zucchini, and squash and cook another 12 minutes, or until the macaroni is tender.

To make *pistou,* puree remaining garlic, cayenne, basil, half the cheese, and tomato in a food processor or blender. Slowly work in the oil and remaining cheese until a coarse sauce is formed.

Place mixture on the table so that each diner can stir a portion into his hot soup before eating.

Serves 8 to 10

3 small beef marrow bones

1½ cups green split peas

1 medium-size onion, cut in half

1 clove garlic

Split Pea Soup
with Pinched Dumplings

1 carrot, shredded

1 potato, cubed

2 stalks celery, cut in half

8 cups cold water

Dumplings:

1 egg, well beaten

1 teaspoon cold water

¼ teaspoon pepper

3 tablespoons (or more) flour

*P*lace bones, peas, and all vegetables in large soup pot with water. Bring to a boil, reduce heat, cover, and simmer gently 2 hours, or until peas are soft. Remove marrow bones, onion, garlic, and celery.

In a small bowl, beat egg and water together with a wire whisk. Add pepper, then flour until a slightly stiff batter forms. Flour fingers and pinch small pieces of dough into a pot of boiling water. Cook 30 minutes. They will float to the top. Test to see if they are cooked through. Remove with a slotted spoon and add to hot split pea soup.

Serves 6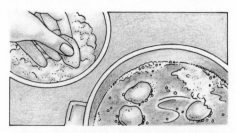

2 tablespoons butter

1 large onion, chopped

6 large, very ripe tomatoes,
    coarsely chopped

4 to 6 basil leaves or ¼ teaspoon
    dried

¼ teaspoon pepper

4 cups Poultry Stock (see Index)

1 cup cooked brown rice

  shredded basil leaves for
    garnish

Tomato
Rice Soup

*M*elt butter in a large, heavy skillet and saute onion until wilted. Add tomatoes, basil, and pepper and simmer, covered, 15 minutes.

Puree in a food mill or press through a sieve to remove tomato skins and seeds.

In a large pot, add stock, tomato pulp, and rice. Heat and serve hot garnished with shredded basil leaves.

Serves 4 to 6

Index